The All-American Slow-Cooker Cookbook

120 Classic All-American Slow Cooker Recipes You'll Never Want to Live Without

Dexter Jackson

Additionally, the information found on the following pages is intended for informational purposes only and should thus be considered, universal. As befitting its nature, the information presented is without assurance regarding its continued validity or interim quality. Trademarks that mentioned are done without written consent and can in no way be considered an endorsement from the trademark holder.

Table of Contents

Introduction

Congratulations on purchasing your personal copy of *The All-American Slow Cooker Cookbook: Classic All-American Slow Cooker Recipes You'll Never Want to Live Without,* and thank you for doing so. You will quickly realize how good it feels to come home at the end of a hard day and relax because you know your meal will be waiting for you in the kitchen!

You might not realize how versatile your Crock Pot is, but its capability to be a slow cooker is only the beginning as you will soon discover. You will have fun making tasty and less time-consuming meals that you and your family will enjoy.

The following chapters will discuss some of the many different ways to cook chicken, beef, potatoes, and all of the other healthy foods that make you proud to say you love the American way of eating! You will discover ways to cook everything from applesauce to zucchini.

You will learn how important it is to use the correct size crock pot indicated for in the recipe. It has been designed with the cooking times in mind. Therefore, if you have a recipe that calls for three hours in the six-quart pot and has a different size, the cooking time can vary. You may need to make some minor adjustments, but it will be a quick fix. Just keep this in the preparation of your delicious recipes.

There are plenty of books on this subject on the market, thanks again for choosing this one! Every effort was made to ensure it is full of as much useful information as possible. Please enjoy!

Chapter 1: Breakfast Delights

You may be very surprised with the huge variety of meals and treats that can be available to you at breakfast with your slow cooker!

1. Boiled Eggs

Did you ever been on your way to bed, and decide you want some boiled eggs or egg salad for breakfast or work tomorrow, but do not have the time to sit around and wait for the eggs to cook? You can fix that!

Ingredients and Instructions

The simplicity is amazing!

1. Pour some water into the slow cooker, add as many eggs as you want, and set the pot for 3 ½ hours on the low setting. Go back to bed and enjoy tomorrow!

2. One-Hour Bread

Ingredients
1 ½ C. Baking Mix
3 Tbsp. Italian Seasoning
½ cup milk {skim is good also}

Optional: ½ C. shredded cheese or 3 Tbsp. Grated Parmesan cheese

Instructions
1. Prepare the cooker with some non-stick cooking spray.
2. Combine all of the ingredients until the lumps are gone and empty into the cooker.

Notes: Bisquick® is a good choice.

3. French Toast Bites

Ingredients
2 loaves refrigerated French loaf {such as Pillsbury}
1 ½ C. whole milk
6 large eggs
1 Tbsp. vanilla
½ C. pure maple syrup
1 C. heavy cream
4 Tbsp. butter
1 tsp. cinnamon
1/3 C. brown sugar
2 C. pecan pieces
4 Tablespoons butter

Instructions
1. Bake the loaf bread following the package instructions.
2. Prepare the cooker with some cooking spray to coat a four to five-quart slow cooker.
3. Slice the bread loaves into ¾-inch cubes. Bake the cubes in a 225°F oven for thirty to forty minutes until it is crispy. Add it to the slow cooker.
4. Combine the maple syrup, cinnamon, milk, cream, eggs, and vanilla in a blender—adding it to the cooker over the bread.
5. In a separate dish, combine the brown sugar, nuts, and butter. Sprinkle over the top of the mixture in the pot.
6. Set the desired time and cover with the lid. Twenty minutes before you serve this tasty treat—remove the top and let the toast cool off and set.
7. Serve with a drizzle of maple syrup and some fresh berries.

Yields: Eight Servings
Preparation time is 30 minutes.
Settings: Low setting for four to five hours

4. Breakfast Grits

Ingredients
½ Cup stone-ground corn grits
2 Cups water
3 Tablespoons pure maple syrup/honey
For serving: Berries or sliced fruit
Pinch of salt

Instructions
1. Combine all of the components in the cooker. Cover and cook for the desired amount of time or overnight. If you are available, you can stir several times during the process with a whisk.
2. Serve with the toppings right before serving—stirring well.

Yields: Four Servings
Settings: Low for 7 to 9 hours

5. Old-Fashioned Oatmeal

Ingredients
4 ¾ cups water
2 cups thick-cut/old-fashioned rolled oats
Pinch of salt

Instructions
1. Toss in all of the ingredients and mix well.
2. Place the lid on the cooker and cook for the desired times.
3. Serve with some cream, milk, or buttermilk. Add a bit of cinnamon, brown sugar, or toasted wheat germ for a tasty start of the day kind of meal.

Variations of Old-Fashioned Oatmeal

Blueberry Oats: Add 1 cup of fresh blueberries during the last thirty minutes of cooking.
Orange Oatmeal: Add two tablespoons of thawed orange juice concentrate and ¼ cup of coarsely chopped candied orange peel to the slow cooker.

Mixed Grain Oatmeal: Add one cup of brown or white rice either and the start of during the last thirty minutes of the cooking cycle, depending on the consistency you desire of the rice.

Yields: Four Servings
Settings: Low for seven to nine hours
High for two to three hours

6. Blueberry Steel Cut Oats

Ingredients
1 ½ C. of water
2 C. frozen blueberries
1 banana
1 C. Steel cut oats
1- ½ C. Vanilla almond milk
1 Tbsp. butter
1 ½ tsp. cinnamon

Instructions
1. Prepare a six-quart cooker with the butter, making sure to cover the sides also.
2. Mash the banana slightly and add all of the ingredients into the cooker—stirring gently.
3. Place the top on the crock pot and cook for *one hour* on the HIGH setting; switch to the WARM setting overnight, and sleep tight!
4. Add a drizzle of honey and get moving!

Servings: Four to Six
Preparation Time: Fifteen Minutes
Cooking Time: Eight hours

7. Pumpkin Pie Oatmeal

Ingredients
1 C. oats {steel cut}
3 ½- C. water
1 C. pumpkin puree
¼ tsp. each:
- salt
- vanilla extract
- pumpkin pie spices

Optional: 2 Tbsp. maple syrup

Instructions
1. Use some non-stick cooking spray to coat the Crock-Pot®.
2. Empty the oats into the Pot.
3. Mix the remainder of the ingredients in a large mixing container, and pour over the oats.
4. *Note*: If you like to enjoy a sweeter oatmeal, consider adding some additional flavoring after it is cooked.

Cooking Time: Eight hours on the low setting

8. Italian Sausage Scramble

Ingredients
1 medium yellow onion
1 ½ Pounds Italian sausage
6 medium red potatoes
¼ Cup fresh Italian minced parsley
1 medium diced tomato
1 Cup frozen/fresh kernel corn
2 cups grated Cheddar cheese

Instructions
1. Discard the outer casing from the sausage. Peel and dice the onions and potatoes.
2. Sauté the onion and crumbled sausage until browned. Place them on a few paper towels to absorb the grease/fat and add the items to the slow cooker.
3. Combine the rest of the ingredients—blending well. Cover and cook.

Servings: Six
Prep Time is 15 Minutes
Cook Time: The high setting is for four hours, and the lower setting is for six to eight hours.

9. Breakfast Fiesta Delight

Ingredients
1 Pound Country-Style Sausage
1 Package {28-ounces} frozen hash brown potatoes {thawed}
½ Cup whole milk
12 large eggs
1 ½ Cups shredded Mexican blend cheese

Instructions
1. Prepare the Crock-Pot® by spraying it with some cooking spray to help with the cleanup.
2. Brown and crumble the sausage in a frying pan. Remove and pat the grease away using a paper towel.
3. Whip the eggs together in a mixing container.
4. Layer the ingredients with a layer of potatoes, cheese, sausage, and eggs.
5. *Serving Time*: Have some salsa, sour cream, pepper, and salt for a tasty topping.

Servings: Six to Eight
Prep Time is fifteen minutes.
Cooking Time is six to eight hours.

10. Tater Tot Casserole

Ingredients
1 Pound browned ground beef
{16-ounces} Package Tater Tots
1 Can Ro*Tel, mild or hot
1 can Cream of Chicken soup
1 small chopped onion
2 Cups cheese {shredded cheddar}

Instructions
1. Prepare the beef and add the chopped onion along with the Ro*Tel.
2. Empty the concoction into the slow cooker. Blend in the soup.
3. Top off the ingredients with the tater tots.

Cooking Time: Low for two to three hours

The Sweets Corner

11. Slow Cooker Apple Butter Delights

Ingredients
15 medium to large Red Delicious apples
3 teaspoons cinnamon
2 Cups sugar

Instructions
1. Peel, core, and slice the apples into wedges. Combine all of the ingredients into the slow cooker.
2. Cook for the predetermined time and remove the top, stirring during the last hour to thicken the butter.
3. You can use an upright blender or immersion blender to cream the butter and bring it to a consistent texture.

Enjoy over some pancakes, biscuits, or over some ice cream.

Yields: Approximately 72 ounces
Settings: High for two hour
Low for six to eight hours

12. Pumpkin Butter with an Instant Pot

This recipe will work with any slow cooker.

Ingredients
1 cup apple juice
4 teaspoons pumpkin pie spice
2 cans pure pumpkin
½ cup sugar
Optional: 1 teaspoon ground ginger

Instructions
1. Put each of the ingredients directly into the Instant Pot.
2. Use the high pressure for three minutes. Allow the butter cool for at least three hours.
3. You can place the cooled product in whatever glass jars you might have on hand. Use a marker to date each of them, and store them in the refrigerator.

13. Pancakes in the Slow Cooker

Who would have ever believed pancakes could be cooked this way?

Ingredients
Pancake Mix: Prepare referring to the box's instructions for the number of people you will feed.
Syrup: 1 Cup for the batter {+} more for the top
Butter for the top

Instructions
1. Prepare the batter with one cup of maple syrup in a large mixing container.
2. Add a drizzle to the top if you like them sweet!

Cooking Times: For a smaller cooker, it is cooked on high for two to three hours. Cooking on low depends on the size of the cooker and the amount of batter used. The times will fluctuate depending on the size of the cooker. It is best to make a trial run.

14. Cinnamon Roll Pancake

Whoever said you can't enjoy cinnamon pancakes in the slow cooker?

Ingredients
2 eggs
2 C. Original Bisquick™ mix
1 C. milk
3 Tbsp. Granulated sugar
1 tsp. cinnamon
1 tsp. vanilla
Non-stick cooking spray

Instructions
1. Blend the milk, Bisquick, vanilla, and eggs in a large mixing container until well combined.
2. Spray a three to four-quart cooker with the non-stick spray. Pour the batter into the cooker.
3. In a separate container, combine the cinnamon and sugar, add to the top of the batter.
4. Swirl the ingredients with a knife/spoon to make the cinnamon swirl pancake.
5. Cook until the pancake is set.

Yields: Four Servings
Settings: High setting for 1 to 1 ½ hours

Chapter 2: Lunch Favorites

15. New York Dirty Hot Dogs

This delicious recipe is designed for an Instant Pot but can be used in a regular slow cooker.

Ingredients
1 quart of water
6 hotdogs {not skinless}
6 hot dog buns
1 Tbsp. White or red vinegar
⅛ Tsp. whole nutmeg {freshly grated}
½ tsp. cumin

Instructions
1) Pour the water, vinegar, nutmeg, and cumin into the Instant Pot/slow cooker.
2) Add the hotdogs and lock the lid, making sure you close the pressure valve.
3) Cook at the lowest pressure setting for three minutes, using the natural release feature.
4) Serve on the buns and have a great lunch and enjoy.

Yields: Three Servings

Beef

16. Beef and Cheddar Sandwiches

Ingredients
2 Pounds beef chuck roast
1 pouch dry onion soup mix
2 C. water
1 ½ C. shredded sharp cheddar cheese
6 Sandwich buns

Instructions
1. It is recommended to use a six-quart slow cooker for this one.
2. Arrange the beef in the cooker and add the soup mix. Empty the water into the pot and cook until done.
3. Transfer the beef to a cutting board and shred. Place it back into the juices.
4. Toast the buns on the broiler, and top with ¼ cup of the cheese on each of the hot buns.

Yields: Six Servings
Preparation Time: Two Minutes
Settings: Eight to Twelve hours on the low setting

17. French Dipped Roast Beef Sandwich

This recipe is fabulous since you can freeze some of it for later. The process used for this recipe is geared toward using an Instant Pot slow cooker. It works the same in any slow cooker.

Ingredients
4 Lbs. Beef roast
1 tsp. beef bouillon granules
¾ cup soy sauce
2 tsp. black peppercorns
1 tsp. minced garlic cloves
1 Tbsp. Dried rosemary

For Serving
8 white hamburger buns

Instructions
1. Cut the bulk of the fat from the roast and place it into the slow cooker.
2. Blend the peppercorns, bouillon, soy sauce, garlic, and rosemary. Empty the mixture into the pot and pour enough water to immerse the roast.
3. Lock the top and close the steam nozzle—set the timer for 35 minutes on high. Release the pressure and shred the roast.

Perfect for Freezing: All you need is some labels and two one-gallon freezer bags. You can mix the bouillon cube, soy sauce, garlic, peppercorns, and rosemary. Pour it over the roast, label, and freeze. Simple as that!

Yields: Eight Servings

18. Beef Tacos {Short Cut}

Ingredients
1 Package taco seasoning
1 (ten-ounce) Can tomatoes and green chilies (Rotel)
1 Pound lean ground beef

Instructions
1. Add everything listed into your Crock-Pot.
2. If you are available, stir every couple of hours to break up the beef or break it up before serving.
3. Serve on a floured tortilla or taco shell with your choice of toppings.

Servings: 12 tacos
Preparation Time: Two Minutes
Cooking Time: Five to Six Hours

19. Taco Meat

Ingredients
2 Pounds ground beef
3 Tbsp. tomato paste
1 Tbsp. chili powder
1 tsp. each:
- Black pepper
- Sea salt
- Cumin

½ tsp. each:
- Onion powder
- Garlic powder
- Dried oregano
- Coriander

¼ tsp. each:
- Crushed red pepper
- Paprika

Instructions
1. Mix all of the spices in a small container.
2. Add to the cooker: tomato paste, beef, and the spices. Use a wooden spoon to break up the meat.
3. Cook on the low setting for four hours.
4. Add to your favorite dish and enjoy!

Note: As a special flavor enhancer, reserve two teaspoons of the taco seasonings to add the last thirty minutes of the cooking cycle.

20. Sloppy Joes

Ingredients
1 ½ Pounds ground chicken
½ yellow onion
2 green bell peppers
½ Tablespoon each:
- Onion powder
- Salt
- Garlic powder

½ teaspoon pepper
1 Cup beef broth
¼ cup ketchup
2 Tablespoons each:
- Worcestershire sauce
- Corn starch

Instructions
1. Brown the chicken in a skillet on the stovetop, add the pepper, salt, garlic and onion powder.
2. Chop the onions and peppers into ¾-inch pieces and add to the chicken sautéing for about one to two minutes.
3. Arrange the onions, peppers, and chicken in the slow cooker
4. Use a jar with a lid and shake the Worcestershire sauce, cornstarch, ketchup, and broth together. Pour it into the cooker.
5. Serve on burger buns with some provolone or pepper jack cheese for a final 'kick.'

Settings: Low for 3 to 4 hours

21. Sausage and Peppers

If you are from the United States, nothing says this recipe like the State Fair!

Ingredients
1 Tablespoon olive oil
½ lb. ground beef
1 lb. sweet sausage {bulk-ground}
1 {8-ounce} Can tomato sauce
2 {15-ounce each} fire roasted tomatoes
1 sliced red pepper
1 small sliced onion
1 sliced green pepper
Sliced Mozzarella or Provolone
Fresh Rolls

Instructions
1. Over medium heat, pour in the oil in a large pan. Brown the beef and sausage.
2. When done, add to the slow cooker, and add the remainder of components except for the cheese and rolls.
3. Cook on the low setting for five to seven hours.
4. When ready, toast the rolls, adding a slice of cheese and brown until the cheese melts.

Add the sausage and enjoy!

Chicken

22. Creamy Chicken Tacos

Ingredients
1 Can Rotel tomatoes
3 boneless chicken breasts
½ brick {4-ounces} cream cheese

Instructions
1. Place the breasts of chicken in the cooker and pour the tomatoes on top.
2. Cook six to eight hours, shredding the chicken about thirty minutes before the end of the cycle. Add the cheese and leave it on the top to melt for the last few minutes.
3. Add your additional components such as tomatoes, cheese, lettuce, cilantro, and sour cream. It is an anything goes kind of meal!

Settings: Low for six to eight hours

23. Chicken Verde

Ingredients
1 Cup Chicken broth
6 to 8 Chicken breasts {no skin or bones}
1 {16-ounces} Jar Tomatillo salsa

Instructions
1. Layer the chicken in the crockpot and cover with the broth and salsa.
2. Cook for six to eight hours and shred with a fork.
3. Mix well and serve as a salad, burrito, quesadilla, or taco.

Settings: Low for 6 to 8 hours

Turkey

24. Chipotle Turkey Barbecue

Ingredients
1 {7-ounces} Can of chipotle peppers in adobo sauce
4 Pounds bone-in turkey – thighs or drumsticks
2 Cups coleslaw mix
1/3 Cup cider vinegar
Optional:
- BBQ sauce
- Pickles

Instructions
1. Arrange the prepared turkey in the slow cooker.
2. Use a chopper/food processor to combine the vinegar, adobo sauce, and peppers. Make the mixture, coarsely chopped, and add it to the top of the turkey parts.
3. Cook to the desired times and transfer the turkey from the crock—reserving the sauce. Let the meat cool a few minutes.
4. Shred the meat and discard the bones and skin. Moisten with the sauce, but remember the sauce is spicy.
5. Add the creation to a slider bun with some pickles and slaw if you wish along with some barbecue sauce

Note: If you have a four-quart cooker, use smaller chicken pieces/parts since the recipe calls for that size.

Settings: Low setting for seven to eight hours or the high setting for three to four hours
Yields: Six to Eight Servings

Pork

25. Pork Barbecue

Ingredients
1 {3 to 4 Pound} Boneless Boston butt shoulder roast
1 {12-ounce} Can Cola soft drink
1 {18-ounce} bottle of barbecue sauce

Instructions
1. Lightly grease a six-quart slow cooker.
2. Empty the sauce and cola over the pork.
3. Cover and cook for eight to ten hours while you sleep or perform your daily activities.
4. Place on a cutting board on the counter and shred with two forks, discarding any large chunks of fat. Remove/skim the fat from the sauce and add the pork to the mixture. Yummy!

Yields: Six to Eight Servings
Preparation Time: 10 minutes
Settings: Low for 8 to 10 hours

26. Root Beer Pulled Pork

Ingredients
1 {3 Pounds} Boneless pork butt
½ cup liquid smoke
3 cups root beer

Instructions
1. Use some cooking spray to coat the cooker, and arrange the roast in the bottom.
2. Pour the liquid smoke and root beer over the chicken and cook for the desired doneness.
3. Serve on some buns with your choice of sauce. Yummy!

Yields: Eight to Ten Large servings
Settings: Low for eight hours
Preparation Time: Ten minutes

Chapter 3: Soups, Sides, Veggies and Casseroles

Soups in the Slow Cooker

27. Bean Soup

An outside source discovered many years ago that this recipe had been used in the kitchens of the United States Senate. Here it is on a smaller scale:

Ingredients
10 Cups water
1 large ham hock
1 Pound Navy beans {soaked overnight}
2 medium minced onions
6 celery ribs {a few leaves too}
¼ teaspoon ground black pepper
⅓ Cup fresh chopped flat-leaf parsley
3 medium baking potatoes
To taste: Salt

Instructions
1. Peel and cube the potatoes. Empty the liquid from the beans and pour them and the ham into the slow cooker with the cold water.
2. Cover the pot and cook for one hour using the high setting. Drain the liquid {be careful}.
3. Add the ten cups of water, ½ of the parsley, potatoes, celery, and onions and choose your setting of eight to ten hours using the low setting.

4. Toss in the pepper, rest of the parsley, salt, and continue cooking on low for 15 more minutes.

5. Transfer the ham hock from the pot to the garbage {or your pooch}, and leave the deliciously tender meat in the soup.

Serve with some garlic bread for that extra 'bit of home.'

28.   Caribbean Beef Stew

Ingredients
1 ½ Pounds Stew Beef
3 C. collard greens
3 Plantains
3 C. water
1 Tablespoon allspice
1 teaspoon each:
- Cayenne pepper
- Chili powder
3 Tablespoons each:
- Garlic powder
- Smoked paprika

Instructions
1. Cut the beef into chunks. Peel the plantains and slice them into bits. Chop the collard greens. Add these ingredients into the slow cooker.
2. Toss all of the rest of the components into the cooker and cook for eight hours.
3. When done, shred the beef or eat it as chunks along with a tasty veggie.

Yields: Six Servings {Paleo favorite}

29.   Crock-Pot® Taco Soup

Ingredients
1 Can kidney beans {16-ounces}
1 {14.5-ounces} Can Each:
- Beef broth
- Petite diced tomatoes

1 {15-ounces} Can Each:
- Black beans
- Corn

1 {10-ounces} Can Ro*Tel Original
1 {1-oz.} pouch each:
- Taco seasoning mix
- Ranch seasoning mix {Hidden Valley}

½ teaspoon salt
1 ½ teaspoons onion powder
1 Lb. Ground beef

Garnish: Sour Cream, Fritos, chopped green onions, or some shredded cheddar cheese

Notes: The recipe is excellent if you choose the 'Diced Tomatoes with Green Chilies.'

Instructions
1. Cook the beef and drain. Rinse and drain all of the cans of veggies except for the chilies. Reserve the liquid from the corn and tomatoes.
2. Toss everything into the Crock-Pot® {except for the garnishes}.
3. Cook for the necessary time. When the process is completed, add the garnishes of your choice with some Fritos on the side to complement the flavors.

Yields: Eight to ten servings
Preparation Time: Ten minutes
Cooking Times: Low setting for 4 hrs.
             High setting for 2 hrs.

Special Instant Pot - Slow-Cooker Soups for Vegetarians

30. Butternut Squash & Curry Soup

Ingredients
2 garlic cloves
1 large chopped onion
1 ½ tsp. sea salt {fine}
1 T. curry powder
1 {3-Pound} Butternut squash
1 tsp. olive oil
½ C. coconut milk/coconut cream
3 C. water

Optional Garnishes:
- Dried cranberries
- Hulled pumpkin seeds

Instructions
1. Cut the squash into one-inch cubes, or use some you have already frozen. Mince the cloves.
2. Use the sauté function and warm the oil. Toss in the onions and sauté approximately eight minutes. Blend in the curry powder and garlic for about a minute.
3. Turn off the Pot. Add the squash, water, and salt. Close the top making sure the seal is also closed.
4. Choose the 'soup' function and let it cook for thirty minutes on the high-pressure setting.
5. You can quick release or wait it out for the ten minutes or so.
6. Pour it from the pot and mix it until smooth using a blender or food processor. Place it back into the Pot and pour in the coconut milk/cream.
7. Top with some dried cranberries, a pinch of salt, and some hulled pumpkin seeds.

Note: The leftovers are good for about one week in the refrigerator.
Yields: Four to Six Servings

31. Indo-Chinese Corn Soup

Ingredients
1 C. minced each minced:
- carrot
- cabbage

2 ½ cups corn kernels
2 t. sesame oil
1 Tbsp. Soy sauce
5 cups vegetable broth
2 tsp. grated ginger
1 ½ -teaspoons ground cumin
2 tsp. minced garlic

Optional Spice: Ground pepper

Instructions
1. Mix all of the components on the list into the Instant Pot—except for the pepper.
2. Use the high-pressure setting for ten minutes. Natural release the pressure on the IP.
3. Use about three cups of the soup and blend to thicken; return it to the pot.
4. Add a pinch of pepper or other flavorings.

Yields: Four servings

32. Instant Pot Saag

This soup is an Indian version of creamed spinach dish that is full of many nutrients. It is even better the second day.

Ingredients
1 Lb. each rinsed:
 mustard leaves

spinach
2 medium carrots
2 medium diced onions
4 minced garlic cloves
1 {2-inch} knob minced ginger
2 Tbsp. Ghee
2 tsp. salt
1 tsp. each:
- Cumin
- Garam masala
- Coriander

Pinch of dried fenugreek leaves
½ tsp. each:
- Black pepper
- Turmeric
- Cayenne

Instructions
1. Program the Instant Pot with the sauté button to melt the ghee.
2. Blend the ginger, garlic, onion, and other spices to the Pot—stirring for about two to three minutes.
3. Toss in the spinach, and continue to stir. As soon as the spinach wilts, add the mustard greens.
4. Push in the 'keep warm-cancel' button, put the lid on, and press the 'poultry' function for fifteen minutes.
5. Once the Instant Pot pressure releases, add the mixture into a blender and mix to the desired consistency.

6. Return it to the pot and push the 'keep warm' function until you are ready to serve dinner.

Garnish with a spoonful of ghee.

Notes: More ghee will be needed for serving. You may also want to add a small amount of corn starch or potato starch to thicken the soup. Add a small amount of the saag in a bowl and cream the starch in by mixing until it is dissolved. Pour it back into the saag and mix it in well. This process should thicken the soup to what you like.

33. Split Pea Soup

Ingredients
1 medium diced sweet potato
5 cups water
½ cup navy beans
1 cup split peas
3 bay leaves
½ teaspoon liquid smoke
Pepper and Salt
¼ - ½ cup nutritional yeast

Instructions
1. Combine the sweet potato, water, split peas, bay leaves, navy beans, and liquid smoke in the Instant Pot.
2. Use the high-pressure function for twenty minutes. Do a natural release.
3. Toss in the pepper, salt, and nutritional yeast. Adjust the seasonings as desired.

Yields: Four to Six Servings

34.   3-Bean Chili

Ingredients
2/3 Cups each:
- Dried red beans
- Pinto beans
- Black beans

OR 1 ½ Cups each of the cooked beans {out of the can: drained}

Saute Ingredients
2 cups chopped onions
1 t. cumin seeds
1 Tbsp. Minced garlic

Add-In Ingredients
3 ½ cups boiling vegetable broth/water
1 (de-seeded and chopped) red bell pepper
¾ cup chopped carrots {2 sticks}
¼ cup celery {1 stick}
1 ½ teaspoon each:
- Cumin
- Dried oregano

2 tablespoons mild chili powder
½ teaspoon coriander
1 teaspoon smoked paprika
Optional: ¼ teaspoon cayenne pepper

After Instant Pot Cooking Ingredients {14.5 oz.} 1 Can each:
- Diced tomatoes
- Tomato sauce

Garnish Suggestions:
- Cashew sour cream
- Fresh parsley
- Choice of hot sauce
- Fresh cilantro

- Nutritional yeast
- Green onions
- Black olives
- Roast red peppers

Instructions

1. Rinse all of the beans, combine, and cover with water. Soaking overnight is best, but for a minimum of eight hours is recommended. Rinse and drain again after soaking.
2. Use the sauté function for five minutes on the Instant Pot. Toss in the onion, cumin seeds, and minced garlic. Add the water/vegetable broth to avoid burning {as needed}.
3. Blend in the remainder of the ingredients, saving the tomato sauce and diced tomatoes for after the cooking cycle. Mix well, lock and secure the lid, with the vent valve closed.
4. Use the high-pressure manual setting for 12 minutes (for six minutes if you used canned beans).
5. Once the 12/6 minutes are completed, allow a natural pressure release.
6. Blend in the can of tomato sauce and paste. Let the lid stay off of the Instant Pot as the chili cools.

Note: If you want a thicker chili than this, blend one to two cups of the chili mixture in a high-speed blender/mixer. Add it back into the Instant Pot.

Garnishes:
Saute 2 cups of chopped onions, 1 teaspoon of cumin seeds with a tablespoon of minced garlic, yummy!

Yields: Six to Eight Servings

35.   Veggie & Lentil Soup

Ingredients
6 small potatoes
1 cup onions (diced)
3 cups chopped broccoli
3 large sliced carrots
2 quarts water
1 cup dry lentils
1 tsp. each:
- Garlic powder
- Salt
- Onion powder

1 bay leaf
½ teaspoon each:
- Black pepper
- Thyme
- Paprika

Instructions
1. Toss all of the chopped vegetables into the Instant Pot.
2. Throw in the lentils after they have been sorted and rinsed.
3. Blend in the seasonings and pour the water into the pot.
4. Close the top, making sure you seal the vent.
5. Use the arrows (-) and (+) to set manually for 15minutes.
6. When the cycle is finished its cycle, you can unplug the unit and let the Instant Pot release the pressure naturally. After 10 minutes, you can release the remainder of the pressure in the pot.
7. Discard the bay leaf and serve.

Noodle Time

36.   Lasagna Enchantment

This one has a few more steps, but it is so worth it—and it's easy.

Ingredients
2 Cans diced tomatoes {28-ounces} drained
Four finely chopped clove of garlic
2 Tbsp. Oregano
½ tsp. salt
15-ounces fresh ricotta
¼ tsp. Pepper
½ tsp. salt
½ C. shredded Parmesan cheese
1 {12-ounce} Package uncooked lasagna noodles
½ tsp. fresh finely chopped} parsley – more if desired
2 C. spinach leaves {packaged is alright for this one}
2 C. shredded Mozzarella cheese

Instructions
1. Mix the garlic, drained tomatoes, pepper, salt, and oregano in a mixing container.
2. In another bowl, blend the parsley, Parmesan, and ricotta cheese.
3. Dip anywhere from 1/3 to ½ cup of the tomato combination on the base of the Crock-Pot®.
4. Layer the noodles, spinach, several dollops of the ricotta combo, and 1/3 to about ½ of the tomato combination. Sprinkle the mozzarella on the top of that section. Continue the process with the mozzarella on the top.
5. Close the top on the Pot and let it do the work.

Servings: Six to Eight
Prep Time: 20 Minutes
Cook Time: High is 2 Hrs. or Low is 3 to 4 Hrs.

37. **Macaroni and Cheese**

Ingredients
1 {12-ounce} can evaporated milk
1 {16-ounce} Box elbow macaroni
4 Tablespoons cubed salted butter
1 ½ Cups Half & Half
¾ Pound block cubed white American cheese
3 Cups {divided} shredded cheddar cheese
¼ teaspoon pepper
½ teaspoon salt
Instructions
1. Prepare the pasta according to package instructions until almost done.
2. Use a bit of non-stick cooking spray to coat the surface of a four-quart slow cooker. Add the butter.
3. Empty the Half & Half, evaporated milk, salt, cubed American cheese, and 2 cups of the shredded cheddar cheese into the cooker. Stir to mix.
4. Place the lid on and cook for the desired amount of time. During the last fifteen minutes, add the rest of the shredded cheese.
5. Cover the pot again and let the cheese melt on the warm cycle.

Preparation Time: 20 Minutes
Cooking Time: Low for 1 ½ to 2 hours {stir occasionally}

38. Beef Stroganoff

Ingredients
1 Jar sliced mushrooms {drained}
2 lbs. Beef stew meat
1 Cup each:
- Condensed Cream of Onion Soup
- Chopped onions
- Condensed Cream of Mushroom Soup

¼ teaspoon pepper
6 Cups cooked noodles
1 {8-ounces} container of sour cream
1 package cream cheese

Instructions
1. Brown the beef in a pan and transfer it to the slow cooker.
2. Pour in both cans of the soup, the pepper, and the onions into the pot.
3. Cook on low for eight to ten hours.
4. Blend in the cheese until it melts, then the sour cream.
5. Mix or serve separately, enjoy!

Chicken, Beef, and Pork Casseroles

39.   Chicken with Mushrooms and Artichokes

It does not get much easier than this!

Ingredients
4 chicken leg quarters
Pepper and Salt
1 Tablespoon Italian Seasoning
1 {6 to 8-ounce} Container sliced mushrooms
½ cup white wine/chicken broth
1 each {8 to 10-ounch} Jar:
- Artichoke hearts
- Kalamata Olives {Drained}

Optional: Fresh parsley

Instructions
1. Dab the chicken dry and flavor with the Italian seasoning, pepper, and salt.
2. Arrange the legs/parts in the cooker. Add the hearts, olives, and sliced mushrooms. Empty the wine/broth over the chicken and veggies.
3. Set the cooker for five hours on the low setting.
4. After that time, transfer the veggies and chicken to an oven-safe dish and broil for ten minutes.
5. Garnish with some parsley. What a treat!

Note: You can also use a whole chicken and cut it into eight pieces.
{Paleo diet friendly}

40.   **Crock-Pot Dinner: Beef or Chicken**

Ingredients
1 Whole/cut up chicken –or– legs and thighs or a Beef Roast
2 Carrots
4 Potatoes
5 Cups water
1 Can celery or cream of mushroom soup {10 ¾ ounce}

Instructions
1. Cut the carrots into four-inch chunks. Put all of the ingredients into the Crock-Pot®.
2. Set the Pot and let it do the work.

Servings: Four
Cooking Time: The high setting will cook the meal in six hours, or you can cook it all day using the low-temperature setting.

Beef Casseroles

41. Swiss Steak Supper

Ingredients
1 ½ Pounds boneless beef round steak
6 to 8 small red potatoes
½ teaspoon peppered seasoned salt
1 ½ cups baby-cut carrots {ready-to-eat}
1 Can un-drained diced tomatoes with Italian herbs {14.5 ounces}
1 medium onion
1 - Jar {12-ounces} Beef gravy
Optional: Fresh parsley

Instructions
1. Slice the beef into six pieces, flavor it with the seasoned salt, and spray a skillet with some oil cooking spray. Cook six to eight minutes on the med-high setting {flipping once} on the stovetop.
2. Quarter the potatoes, chop the parsley, and slice the onions. Add them to a four to five-quart cooker along with the beef.
3. In a separate container, combine the gravy and tomatoes. Spoon over the ingredients in the cooker.
4. Place the lid on the pot and cook.

Yields: Six Servings
Settings: Low heat for seven to eight hours is sufficient.

Veggies

42.   Bourbon Baked Beans

If you are not sure how to cook for the picnic or the Super Bowl, here is the secret!

Ingredients
10 slices thick-cut bacon
1 pound dry navy beans
1 medium chopped sweet onion
2 Cups water
1 minced garlic clove
¾ Cup of your choice - BBQ sauce
¼ Cup ketchup
2 Tablespoons molasses
1 Cup loosely packed brown sugar
1 ½- Tablespoons ground mustard
1 Cup of bourbon {and 1 shot for you}
¼ Cup Apple Cider Vinegar
2 Tablespoons Worcestershire sauce

Instructions
1. Soak the beans overnight and drain in the morning. Put them in a pot of water to simmer for thirty to forty minutes.
2. In a large skillet, over medium temperature, cook the bacon until crispy. Render the fat and remove the bacon to drain on a towel. Cut it into pieces.
3. Lower the heat to med-low and toss in the onion sautéing for eight to ten minutes until soft and caramelized. Add the garlic, cooking for 30 seconds, turn off the burner.
4. Blend in the rest of the ingredients along with the saved bacon fat to the slow cooker and combine. Cook for ten to twelve hours, then turn the cooker to the warm setting or shut it off for thirty minutes to two hours.
5. The longer they sit, they thicker and better they will be, especially the next day for the game.

Yields: Serves 6 to 8

43.   Corn on the Cob

Ingredients
3 whole ears or 5 to 6 halves – Corn on the cob
Salt as needed
1/2 stick or ¼ cup of softened butter

Instructions
1. Shuck and remove the silks from the corn, breaking them into halves.
2. Cover each one with butter and wrap individually in foil.
3. Wad some foil balls up in the base of the unit and add about one-inch of water.
4. Put the potatoes into the Crock-Pot®, and cook for the allotted time.

Yields: Four Servings

Preparation Time: Five minutes
Cooking Time: Use the high setting for two hours.
Note: The cooking time may vary if you prepare the corn with another unit besides a 5 to 6-quart pot.

44.   Ranch Mushrooms

Ingredients
½ Cup Melted butter
1 Pound fresh mushrooms
1 Package ranch salad dressing mix

Instructions
1. Leave the mushrooms whole and wash them well.
2. Put them into the slow cooker, adding the oil and ranch mix by drizzling it over the mushrooms.
3. Cover the cooker. It is best to stir once after hour one to blend the butter.

Yields: Six servings
Cooking Time: Low will have your mushrooms ready in three to four hours.

45. **Stuffed Banana Peppers**

Ingredients
1 Package Italian Sausage
Banana Peppers
2 Jars of Marinara Sauce {approximately}

Instructions
1. Adapt this for your crowd on the amounts used.
2. Remove both ends of the peppers and scoop out the seeds and discard them.
3. Pour ½ of the jar of sauce in the Crock-Pot®.
4. Dice the sausage, in case it is not already prepared.
5. Stuff the pepper with the sausage and put them into the Pot.
6. Pour the sauce over the banana peppers.

Cooking Time: Low for eight to nine hours

46.   Slow Cooked Baked Potatoes

Ingredients
6 Baking Potatoes
Kosher Salt
Oil
Garnishes: Your choice

Directions
1. Prepare the potatoes with a good scrub and rinsing, but do not dry them.
2. Put each one in some foil while poking holes in each one using a fork.
3. Use a small amount of oil to drizzle over each one adding a sprinkle of salt, and close the foil.
4. To keep them from getting soggy, ball up several wads of foil into the cooker.
5. Layer the potatoes on the balls and cover. Leave them on warm in the Crock-Pot® until ready to serve.

Cooking Time: Low – Six to Eight Hours

47. **Sweet Potatoes**

Ingredients
4 medium sweet potatoes
Optional Garnishes:
Brown sugar, butter, mini marshmallows

Instructions
1. Clean and prepare the potatoes—thoroughly dry. Wrap each one in a double liner of foil. Use a fork and poke holes in each one.
2. Arrange them in the Crock-Pot®, cooking them the specified amount of time. If you are close to the kitchen, turn and flip the potatoes in the pot occasionally.
3. Once they are done, add the garnishes of your choice and serve.

Yields: Four Servings

Preparation Time: Five Minutes
Cooking Time: The Low setting is used for eight hours or the high setting for four hours. {Times may vary depending on the size of the potatoes, but you will know when they are ready by how soft the potato is when you give it a squeeze.}

48.   Sweet Potato Casserole

Ingredients
1 ½ C. applesauce
1 tsp. ground cinnamon
3 Tbsp. Margarine/butter
½ C. - Toasted chopped nuts
2/3 C. Brown sugar
6 medium sweet potatoes

Instructions
1. Peel and slice the potatoes cutting them into ½-inch bits and drop them into a 3 ½-quart Crock-Pot.
2. In a separate dish, mix the brown sugar, cinnamon, melted butter, and applesauce. *Note*: Be sure you pack the brown sugar tight when it is measured.
3. Empty the mixture over the potatoes in the Pot. When the potatoes are tender, you can top with the chopped nuts. Tasty!

Cooking Time: Six to Eight hours

Chapter 4: Dinner Favorites

49.   Corned Beef

Ingredients
4 carrots
6 red skin potatoes
4 Pounds Corned beef brisket {uncooked}
1 seasoning packet {note}
6 Cups water

Instructions
1. Combine all of the ingredients into the cooker for eight hours using the high setting. {Paleo favorite}

Note: If there is not a seasoning packet with the brisket, make your own using three tablespoons of pickling spices.

50.   Corned Beef and Cabbage

Ingredients
½ head of cabbage
10 quartered baby red potatoes
4 Cups water
1 onion
4 Pounds beef brisket {with spice package}
6 ounces beer

Instructions
1. Coarsely chop the cabbage, and peel the onion to chop.
2. Arrange the potatoes and onions in the bottom of the cooker, dump the water, and add the brisket.
3. Pour the beer over the meat. Sprinkle with the spices and set to high for eight hours.
4. Stir in the cabbage one hour before the end of the cycle.

Have the rest of the beer and enjoy!

Beef

51. Beef Burgundy with Noodles

Ingredients
1 ½ Pounds Beef stewing beef meat
1 {10 - ¾ ounces} Can of undiluted condensed golden mushroom soup
4 medium carrots
1 large onion
½ Pound whole fresh mushrooms
¼ Cup quick-cooking tapioca
½ Cup Burgundy wine/beef broth
¼ teaspoon each:
  • Pepper
  • Dried thyme
½ teaspoon salt
Egg noodles – cooked & hot

Instructions
1. Cut the meat into one-inch cubes, cut the mushrooms in half, chop the carrots, and cut the onion into thin wedges.
2. Add everything into the five-quart cooker {except for the noodles}.
3. Place the lid on the pot, and cook for five or six hours at the low setting.
4. Serve up with the noodles.

Yields: Six Servings

52.   Beef Tips

This is just too easy!

Ingredients
3 Pounds Stewing beef
1 Can each Cream of:
- Onion soup
- Mushroom soup

Instructions
1. Mix the two cans of soup in the crockpot. Toss in the beef and stir.
2. Place the top on the cooker, and set it on high for four to six hours or using the low setting for six to eight hours.
3. Add some cooked carrots or peas to the cooker for twenty minutes at the end of the cycle.
4. Serve the tasty dish over potatoes, noodles, or rice.

53.   Meatloaf: Turkey or Beef

Can you remember when Grandma made it like this?

Ingredients
1 lb. lean ground turkey or beef
1 Cup quick-cooking oatmeal
1 Can {8-ounces} tomato sauce
1/8 teaspoon pepper
2 Tablespoons dried onion or ½ Cup freshly diced onion
1 teaspoon salt
Barbecue sauce

Instructions
1. Make the mixture for the meatloaf using the tomato sauce, turkey/beef, pepper, salt, oatmeal, and onion. {It is okay to use your hands.}
2. Use an oblong pan and place a loaf pan inside the cooker. Cook for the designated time.
3. After that time, brush the top with some BBQ sauce and put it in the oven on broil for 2 or 3 minutes.

Yields: Four Servings
Settings: An oval slow cooker is necessary for four hours on high or six hours on the low setting.

54.   Mississippi Roast

1 {3-Pound} Chuck Roast
½ Cup {1 stick} margarine or butter
5 to 6 pepperoncini
1 each {1-ounce pouch}:
- Au Jus mix
- Dry ranch Dressing

Instructions
1. Arrange the roast in the slow cooker and sprinkle with the two pouches, the cup of butter, and lastly the pepperoncini.
2. Cook for eight hours on the low setting.
3. Shred the roast and serve with the juicy gravy.

The roast meat tends to be a little salty, so serve over some mashed potatoes or noodles.

55.   Steaks in the Pot

Ingredients
4 to 6 steaks
¼ C. White Wine
2 T. A-1 Sauce
2 T. Dijon mustard

Instructions
1. Blend the mustard and steak sauce, add it to each of the pieces of steak.
2. Add the meat into the Crock-Pot®, add the wine, and cook for six to eight hours.

Servings: Four or More
Cooking Time: Six to eight hours on the low setting

56.   Steak Pizzaiola

Ingredients
1 {one to two pounds} London broil
1 Yellow, orange, or red sliced bell pepper
1 Large sliced onion
¼ Cup water
½ to ¾ of a jar {your choice} tomato pasta sauce

Instructions

1. Flavor the meat with the pepper and salt and place it into the slow cooker.
2. Add the peppers and onions, followed by your favorite sauce.
3. Cook for six to eight hours. {Flip a time or two if you are close by the pot.}
4. Serve over some pasta, potatoes, or veggies.

Cooking Time: Low heat for six to eight hours

Chicken

57. Barbecue Chicken

Ingredients
4 Chicken breasts
1 {18-Ounce} bottle of BBQ sauce
½ can or bottle root beer/ Dr. Pepper/Coke {full sugar}
¼ teaspoon each pepper and salt

Instructions
1. Arrange the breasts and drink of choice in the cooker for the three hours.
2. Drain most of the liquid and shred the chicken, adding the pepper and salt.
3. Empty the sauce into the mix of chicken and cook for about fifteen or twenty minutes.
4. Serve on some rolls. You can always add some sautéed onion or avocado to the sandwich for a change of pace.

Settings: High for 3 hours

58.   Beer and Barbecue Chicken

Ingredients
3 Pounds {6 large no skin or bones} Chicken Breasts
1 teaspoons garlic powder
1 Tablespoon each:
- Smoked paprika
- Onion powder

½ teaspoon pepper and salt
1 {32-ounce} Bottle BBQ sauce
1 {8-ounce} bottle/can beer {classic amber is good}

Instructions
1. Arrange the chicken in the crockpot, flavoring it with the pepper salt, powder, onion, and garlic powder, then— add the beer, along with about 24 ounces of the barbecue sauce.
2. Toss once or twice while cooking for eight hours on the low setting.
3. At that point, shred the chicken, and add the remainder of the sauce.
4. Toss it again and let it rest for ten to fifteen minutes.

Freeze what you don't use today!

Yields: Eight to Ten servings

59. Buffalo Chicken

Ingredients
3 to 5 Pounds Boneless – Skinless Chicken Breasts
1 pouch Hidden Valley Ranch dressing mix
1 {12-ounce} bottle buffalo sauce

Instructions
1. Arrange the breasts in the crockpot. Empty the sauce over the chicken and sprinkle the ranch on top.
2. Cover the pot and cook for approximately five hours.
3. Do not discard the sauce and transfer the chicken to a cutting board. It should fall off the bone.
4. Add it back to the slow cooker and stir to coat the chicken.
5. Cook for another hour or so until the chicken has absorbed the tasty sauce.

Settings: Low for 5 hours {+} 1 hour

60. Butter Ranch Chicken

Ingredients
1 Pouch Hidden Valley ranch mix
4 Chicken breasts
½ stick butter

Instructions
1. Arrange the chicken breasts on the bottom of the crockpot and sprinkle with the ranch mixture.
2. Cut the butter into about eight chunks and place it on top of the mix.
3. Cook until done.

Settings: Low for four to six hours

61. Chicken Stock

You never know when you are going to need some fresh chicken stock. Here is one you need to remember:

Ingredients
1 medium {quartered} onion
1 chicken carcass
3 quartered celery stalks
3 quartered carrots
Water to cover the chicken
1 Tablespoon apple cider vinegar

Instructions
1. Add all of the components for the stock into a slow cooker/crock pot.
2. Strain the final product and freeze or refrigerate.

Cook Time: 12 to 18 hours {Paleo Favorite}

62.   Crock Pot Chicken

Ingredients
1 {3 to 5 Pounds} Chicken

Suggested Options:
- Paprika
- Garlic
- Olive oil
- Rosemary

Instructions
1. Remove the chicken from the package—making sure you remove all of its 'innards' as well as any fat. Rinse and dry entire chicken dry with a towel. Place it in the cooker breast side down.
2. Throw the paper towels away and wash your hands.
3. Give the bird a drizzle of olive oil and a dab with the garlic cloves or rosemary.
4. Turn on the cooker using the low setting for seven hours {more or less}. It should be 165°F if tested with a meat thermometer.
5. Add some peas and potatoes for a delicious meal.

This recipe is another Paleo diet favorite.

63.   Creamy Chicken with Biscuits

Ingredients
1 ½ Pounds {about 8 pieces with no bones or skin} chicken thighs
2 stalks celery {thinly sliced}
3 to 4 carrots {chopped}
1 small onion {chopped}
1 ½ - tsp. ground thyme
¼ C. all-purpose flour
2 tsp. ground sage
½ tsp. each:
- Black pepper
- Ground nutmeg

1 tsp. kosher salt
1 C. each:
- chicken broth
- frozen peas

½ C. heavy cream
6 homemade biscuits or store bought

Instructions
1. Combine the black pepper, thyme, nutmeg, and sage in a small dish.
2. Add the carrots, flour, onions, and celery to the cooker.
3. Place the chicken on top and sprinkle with the ½ teaspoon of the salt and seasonings mixture {step 1}.
4. Cook for the allotted amount of time, for the last 30 minutes make the biscuits.
5. Around ten minutes before dinner: Pour in the cream and the peas with the remaining ½ teaspoon of salt. Combine and heat thoroughly.
6. Split a biscuit in half and enjoy with the mixture over the top.

Yields: Six Servings
Settings: Low setting for five to six hours or the high setting for two and one-half to three hours

64. Biscuits for the Chicken {Above}

Chicken is never quite the same without some homemade biscuits!

Ingredients
½ Cup cold butter {small pieces}
1 teaspoon kosher salt
2 cups all-purpose flour
1 Tablespoon baking powder
1 Cup whole milk

Instructions
1. Preheat the oven temperature to 400°F.
2. Mix the salt, baking powder, and flour in a mixing dish.
3. Use a pastry blender or your hands to meld the butter into the flour until it crumbles into small clumps.
4. Pour in the milk until moist.
5. Drop the mounds on a baking tin and bake for 18 to 20 minutes.

Yields: Six biscuits
Total Time: 35 minutes

65.   Caesar Chicken

Ingredients
1 bottle {12-ounces} Caesar dressing
4 breasts {no bones or skin} chicken
½ C. shredded Parmesan cheese

Instructions
1. Add the breasts of chicken to the Crock-Pot®.
2. Cook the chicken for the specified time and drain the juices.
3. Empty the dressing over the breasts.
4. Sprinkle the cheese on top of that and cook for thirty more minutes covered until done.

Have a side of Caesar salad to complement the meal.

Servings: Four
Prep Time: 5 minutes
Cooking Times: Low for 6 hrs.
                 High for 3 hrs.

66.   Chicken and Dumplings

Ingredients
4 chicken breasts {no skin or bones}
2 {32-ounces} Containers chicken broth or homemade chicken
stock {above}
1 to 2 Cans {10-count} of refrigerated biscuits

Instructions
1. The larger oval slow cooker is recommended for this recipe.
2. Using the high heat setting, empty the stock/broth into the pot.
3. Cut up the breasts into small morsels and add them to the cooker for two hours.
4. When the chicken is done, slice each of the biscuits into two to three pieces {the dumplings}.
5. Add them to the pot. When the biscuits float to the top, push them back into the broth to keep them from sticking together. Continue cooking on high with the lid on for another thirty minutes.
6. Take off the lid and stir, cooking for another twenty minutes uncovered.

Prep Time: Fifteen minutes
Cook time: Three hours

67.   Chicken and Mushroom Gravy

Ingredients
4 to 6 chicken thighs {skinless & boneless}
1 packet onion soup mix
1 Can {13.75-ounces} Cream of mushroom soup

Instructions
1. Frozen or thawed chicken is okay to be placed into the cooker. Sprinkle with the soup mix.
2. Use a spoon to add the soup over the chicken and mix.
3. Cook for the desired times and remove it from the cooker.
4. Shred the chicken and serve it with some rice and gravy or toast. Yummy!

Yields: Four Servings
Settings: Low for 4 to 6 hours

68.   Cranberry Chicken

Ingredients
4 {no skin or bones} Chicken Breasts
1 {8-ounces} bottle Kraft Catalina dressing
1 Pouch dry onion soup
1 {14-ounces} Can Ocean Spray Whole Cranberry Sauce

Instructions
1. Cook the chicken in the slow cooker according to your specified times. Drain the juices.
2. Combine the onion soup mix, cranberry sauce, and dressing. Empty it over the chicken.
3. Cook—covered—about 30 minutes.

Yields: Four Servings
Preparation Time: Five minutes
Use the high setting for three hours or low for six hours.

69.   French Onion Chicken

Ingredients
4 Chicken breasts {no bones or skin}
1 Can French Onion soup {10.5-ounces}
½ cup sour cream

Instructions
1.   Put the breasts in the slow cooker and cook for the stated time. Empty the liquids.
2.   Combine the soup and sour cream and add into the pot on top of the chicken breasts.
3.   Cook covered for about 30 minutes.

Servings: Four
Preparation Time: Five Minutes
Cooking Time: The high setting will take approximately three hours, whereas the low setting takes six hours.

70.   Hawaiian Chicken

Ingredients
4 to 5 skinless and boneless breasts of chicken {thawed}
1 {20-oz.} -Can Dole Pineapple Chunks
1 - Bottle {12-oz.} Heinz Chili Sauce
1/3 C. brown sugar

Instructions
1.   Cook the chicken until its predetermined time limit is completed. Empty the liquid.
2.   Combine the brown sugar, ½ of the juices of the can of pineapples, the chili sauce, and the chunks of pineapple.
3.   Empty the mixture over the drained breasts and heat on the high setting for approximately 30 minutes or so.
4.   Have a bit of pineapple in every bite. Yummy!

Servings: Four to Five
Preparation Time: 5 min.
Cooking Time: High = 6 hrs. / Low = 3 hrs.

71. Honey Mustard Chicken

Ingredients
1 – {12-ounces} Bottle Dijon mustard
1/3 C. honey
4 skinless & boneless chicken breasts {thawed}

Instructions
1. Cook the chicken for its allotted time and dispose of the juices.
2. Combine the mustard and honey in a small dish.
3. Empty the sauce over the chicken and cook for about ½ hour {covered} until done.

Servings: Four
Preparation Time: Five Minutes
Cooking Time: Use the low setting for six hours or on high for three hours.

72.　　Italian Style Chicken

Ingredients
4 chicken breasts {thawed – no bones- no skin}
1 {16-ounces} Bottle Italian Dressing

Instructions
1. Place the breasts of chicken into your Crock-Pot® and pour the dressing on them.
2. Put the lid on and let it do your work!

Servings: Four
Preparation Time: 5 minutes
Cooking Time: Use the high setting to prepare the chicken for 3.5 hrs. Or use the low setting for 7 hours.

73.   Mexican Chicken

Ingredients
3 to 4 chicken breasts {skinless and boneless}
1 {1-ounce} Pouch taco seasoning
1 {14-ounces} Can diced tomatoes with green chilies {Ro*Tel is good}

Instructions
1. Use some cooking spray to coat the slow cooker.
2. Arrange the breasts in the bottom of the cooker and dump in the remainder of the ingredients.
3. Cook for the allotted time and transfer the chicken to a cutting board to shred.
4. Add the chicken back into the cooker and add the tomatoes, mixing well.

   You can use this for nachos, burritos, or on tacos.

Yields: Four to Five Servings
Settings: Cook on high for four to six hours {no longer or the chicken will become dry}, or cook on high for two to three hours.

74.   Orange Soda Chicken

Ingredients
1 Can diet orange soda
4 to 5 Chicken breasts
1/3 Cup soy sauce

Instructions
1. Use a large freezer bag to combine the soy sauce, soda, and chicken.
2. Refrigerate overnight.
3. Serve with a dish of rice.
Settings: Cook on low for six to eight hours.

75.   **Rotisserie-Style Chicken**

You will need an oval slow cooker for this recipe.

Ingredients
1 {3 to 4 pounds} Whole chicken
2 tsp. chili powder
2 Tbsp. packed brown sugar
2 tsp. salt

Instructions
1. Use a five-quart cooker and spray it with some cooking spray.
2. Mix the salt, brown sugar, and chili powder in a small dish.
3. Use some paper towels to dry off the chicken and rub it down with the sugar mixture. Arrange the chicken—breast side upwards—in the cooker, and cover.
4. Cook until the legs easily move when twisted and the inside thigh reaches 165°F.
5. Let the bird rest for ten minutes before slicing.

Yields: Six servings
Settings: Ten minutes preparation time
        High heat setting for 2 ½ to 3 ½ hours

76.   Sweet and Sour Chicken

Ingredients
1 {22-ounces} Bag frozen Tyson Chicken Breast
2 Cups cooked rice/steamed vegetables {or both}
1 bottle {18-ounces} Apricot Preserves
1 jar {12-ounces} chili sauce

Instructions
1. Layer the frozen chicken pieces into the Crock-Pot®.
2. Combine the preserves and chili sauce in a small container {a mixing cup is ideal}. Empty it over the chicken. *Note:* You can also use pineapple or a combination.
3. Toss to mix and let the Pot do the work.
4. Enjoy with some veggies and rice.

Servings: Six {one cup per serving}
Cooking time on the high setting is 2 to 3 hours.

77.   Swedish Meatballs

Ingredients
1 {12-ounce} jar Heinz Home-Style Gravy {Savory Beef}
1 {eight-ounce} container of sour cream
1 Bag Frozen Meatballs

Instructions
1. Empty the gravy into the Crock-Pot®, followed by the sour cream.
2. Combine these until they are completely blended.
3. Toss the package of frozen meatballs into the Pot filling to approximately 2/3 to ¾ of the space.
4. Place the lid on the pot and cook—occasionally stirring if you happen to be close to the kitchen.
5. You can always make more or less of the recipe depending on how many people you will serve.

Cooking Time: Low for a minimum of 5 hours

78. **Teriyaki Chicken**

You will discover this as a loved and much-used recipe for your slow cooker. This teriyaki is also friendly for your Paleo diet plan.

Ingredients
2 pounds {pasture raised} chicken drumsticks
Pepper and salt
½ Cup Teriyaki sauce {see note}
1 teaspoon sesame seeds

Instructions
1. Flavor the drumsticks with the pepper and salt, place them in the slow cooker.
2. Empty the sauce over the chicken and cook for five hours on low.
3. Transfer them from the pot and place them in an oven-safe dish to broil for five minutes.
4. Drizzle the finished drumsticks with the sesame seeds and enjoy!

   Note: You can use Coconut Secret Aminos {found at Wal-Mart, and similar stores}.

Turkey

79.   Stuffed – Roasted Turkey

Ingredients
2 C. Stuffing Mix
Black pepper and salt
6 Pounds Turkey
1 Tablespoon melted butter

Instructions
1. Use the package instructions to prepare the stuffing.
2. Flavor the turkey with some melted butter, pepper, and salt.
3. Prepare the bird by loosely placing the stuffing in the carcass.
4. Cover and let the pot do the rest.

Servings: Four

Cooking Time: Low: 9 to 11 hours
         High: 5 hours

Fish

80.   Citrus Flavored Fish

Ingredients
Pepper and Salt
1 ½ pounds fish fillets
1 medium chopped onion
4 tsp. oil
5 Tbsp. Chopped parsley
2 tsp. Each grated: lemon and orange rind
Garnish: Lemon and orange slices

Instructions
1. Use some butter to grease the Crock-Pot®.
2. Flavor the fish with some pepper and salt and put it into the pot.
3. Add the parsley, grated rinds, and onion as well as the oil over the fish.
4. Cover and cook.
5. When ready to eat, garnish with some lemon or orange slices.

Cooking Time: 1 ½ Hours on Low

81.   Lemon Pepper Tilapia with Asparagus

Ingredients
4 to 6 frozen or thawed Tilapia fillets
1 asparagus bundle
8 to 12 Tablespoons lemon juice
½ Tablespoon butter for each of the fillets
Lemon pepper seasoning

Instructions
1. Prepare a piece of foil for each of the fillets. Add the asparagus to each of the foil pieces.
2. Next, add the fillet followed by the seasonings and a pat of butter to each of the packs.
3. Top off with more asparagus.
4. Fold the foil over each of the units and place them in the cooker for two hours on high for thawed fish or three hours for frozen fish.

82.　　　**Salmon Bake**

Ingredients
3 {one-pound} Cans Salmon
1 {16-ounces} can tomato puree
4 cups bread crumbs {10 slices worth}
1 chopped green pepper
3 teaspoons lemon juice
2 crushed chicken bouillon cubes
1 Can each {condensed}:
    1. Cream of onion soup
    2. Cream of celery soup
6 {beaten} eggs
½ cup milk

Instructions
1. Use some cooking spray or other oil to grease the slow cooker lightly.
2. Blend all of the ingredients—except for the milk and celery soup into the cooker. Cover and cook.
3. Combine and stir the milk and celery soup in a small pan to use as a sauce for the salmon.
4. When the salmon is done, garnish and enjoy with the special sauce!

Cooking Time: High for three hours or low for four to six hours

83.   Shrimp Scampi

Ingredients
1 Pound {16 to 20} raw shrimp thawed
½ Cup white wine
2 Tablespoons olive oil
1/4 Cup chicken broth
2 teaspoons each:
- Minced parsley
- Chopped garlic

Instructions
1. Add everything to the crockpot—adding the shrimp last.
2. *Note:* The ratio should be ½ cup of wine to ¼ cup of broth to each pound of shrimp.
3. Place the top on the pot and cook for 1 ½ hours on high or 2 ½ hours on low.
4. To serve, transfer the shrimp to a bowl and pour the mixture over each of them.

Pork

84.   BBQ Style Pork Steaks

Ingredients
4 {½-inch cut} Pork shoulder steaks
2 large sliced tomatoes
1 large onion
1 large thinly sliced bell pepper
1 tbsp. each:
- Vegetable oil
- Tapioca {use the quick cooking}

¼ C. red wine
½ tsp. cumin
½ C. barbecue sauce {of your choosing}

Instructions
1. Slice and cut the onion as if you are preparing to make onion rings for dinner.
2. Trim away an excess fat and slice the steaks in half - lengthwise.
3. Brown the steaks in skillet using hot oil, and drain on paper towels.
4. Organize the peppers, tomatoes, and onions in the Crock-Pot sprinkling the tapioca over them. Place the pork in last.
5. Prepare the cumin, wine, and barbecue sauce in a small dish. Pour it over the ingredients in the Pot, and cover.

Note: The recipe is based on a 3 ½- or a 4-quart Crock-Pot. If you have a different size the cooking time may vary.

Servings: Four
Cooking Time: Low Heat – Six to Eight Hours {or until veggies and meat are tender}

85.   Maple Orange Pork Shoulder

If you are using the Paleo guidelines, this is super for you!

Ingredients
2 ½ to 3 Pounds - Pork Shoulder
½ cup fresh squeezed orange juice
1 apple
1 tsp. sea salt
1 Tbsp. 100% pure maple syrup
1/2 tsp. each:
- Black pepper
- Dried sage

Instructions
1. Peel and chop the apple. Cut the shoulder into several large chunks to fit into the cooker. Rub each one with the sage, pepper, and salt and add them to the cooker.
2. Toss in the apples, maple syrup, and orange juice.
3. Cook for six hours on the low setting. Pull apart with two forks and enjoy!

86.   **Pastured Pork Shoulder**

Ingredients
1 {4 to 6 Pound} pork shoulder
½ Cup water/bone broth
Fresh ground black pepper
Unrefined sea salt
Organic garlic powder

Instructions
1. Use the garlic powder, pepper, and salt to flavor the pork. Arrange it in the slow cooker.
2. Empty the water/broth in the cooker. Cook on high for one hour. Lower the heat and cook for six to eight hours—depending on the size of the shoulder.
3. Transfer the meat to a container and mix with your favorite BBQ sauce. Reserve the juices for a next recipe or boil it down as a sauce to pour over the pork.

Note: The bone broth is available at superstores such as Wal-Mart unless you decide to make it from scratch. {Paleo-friendly recipe}

87.   Pepsi® Roast

Ingredients
1 Can Cream of mushroom soup
5 Lb. Pork Roast/ Steak/Chops
½ package dry onion soup mix
1 can Regular Pepsi {Do not use Diet}

Instructions
1. Put the meat in the Crock-Pot® first and sprinkle with the soup mix.
2. Empty the mushroom soup and Pepsi over the meat.
3. Close the lid and let the pot do the rest of the chore.
4. Use the sauce to pour over some rice or potatoes.

Servings: Eight
Cooking Time: Low setting for six to seven hours

88.   Ranch Pork Chops

Ingredients
1 Pouch of Ranch Seasoning Dry Mix
6 Pork Chops
1 Can Cream of Chicken soup {plus} 1 - Can of water if needed

Instructions
1. Mix the three ingredients and mix well.
2. Add the water to the mixture if needed if it gets too thick.

Settings: Low 2 to 6 hours {Cooked to 145F similar to chicken breast} or High 3 to 6 hours {can cut with a fork}

89.   Squash 'N Chops

Ingredients
5 Pork (boneless) Pork cutlets or chops
2 medium oranges
1 ¼ Pounds delicate/butternut squash
½ tsp. Garlic salt
1/8 tsp. Ground red pepper
¼ tsp. Each: Ginger, cloves, and cinnamon

Instructions
1. Peel and slice the oranges. Peel and cut the squash lengthwise and discard the seeds. Cut the 'half' into sections ½-inches thick.
2. Flavor the pork with some garlic salt and red peppers. Use a 4 to 5- quart Crock-Pot® and place the chops/cutlets in the bottom.
3. Combine the ginger, cinnamon, and cloves in a small dish.
4. Top off the pork with the oranges along with the toppings in step 3.
5. Cover and cook.

Servings: Five
Cooking Time: Low for 4 hours

90.   Sweet Pork

Ingredients
1 {16-ounces} Jar Salsa {2 Cups}
1 Cup brown sugar
1 {2-Pound} Boneless Pork roast

Instructions
1. Use a six-quart slow cooker and arrange the roast in the bottom along with the mixture of brown sugar and salsa.
2. Pull the pork apart and serve it right away if you desire or let it cool off for another hour or two.

Settings: High for four to five hours / low seven to eight hours

91. Maple Pineapple Ham

Ingredients
2 Cups pineapple juice
7-Pound ham
½ C. Maple syrup
1 C. brown sugar

Instructions
1. Take the ham out of the wrapper and put it into the slow-cooker.
2. Use the brown sugar to rub down each side, pour the juice over the meat along with the maple syrup.
3. Cover and cook four to five hours. {Time is based on a 5- or 6-quart cooker.}
4. With about one hour left, pour some of the juices over the ham.
5. Transfer the meat and let it rest for around ten minutes before serving.

92.   Ham with Cider Gravy

Ingredients
1 {one to four pounds} Ham
¾ cup maple syrup
2 cups unsweetened apple cider
3 Tablespoons cornstarch

Instructions

1. Arrange the ham in the Crock-Pot® and top it off with the syrup and cider.
2. Cook until the time indicated below is completed.
3. Transfer the ham to a serving dish. Pour the liquid into a large cup {a measuring cup is perfect}.
4. Whisk ½ of the cider and the cornstarch on the stovetop using the low-temperature setting until it is smooth. Continue whisking and increase the burner to med-low—adding small amounts of cider at a time—until the gravy is bubbly and thickened to the desired consistency.

Servings: Four to Eight
Preparation Time: Four minutes
Cooking Time: Low - six to eight hours

Chapter 5: Desserts & Appetizers

93.   Applesauce

Ingredients
12 Apples
1 teaspoon juice {plus} -¼ of the lemon peel
2 cinnamon sticks

Instructions
1. Peel, core, and slice the apples. Put the apples, lemon peel, and sticks into the Crock-Pot®.
2. Give it a drizzle to the top with the juice and set the cooking timer.
3. When the applesauce is ready, throw the lemon peel and cinnamon sticks into the trash.
4. Blend with a regular or immersion blender. Chill for a few hours.

Cooking Time is five to seven hours.

94. Apple Crisp

Ingredients
8 apples {peeled and cored}
¼ Cup white sugar
½ to 1 teaspoon cinnamon
½ Cup butter
¾ Cup each:
- Brown sugar
- Oatmeal
- Flour

Instructions
1. Use some cooking spray to prepare the slow cooker.
2. Thinly slice the apples and sprinkle with the sugar and cinnamon. Add to the slow-cooker.
3. Combine the brown sugar, oatmeal, and flour in a medium dish. Use a pastry blender to cut in the butter to achieve a pea-sized crumble. Add to the cooker.
4. Cover the apples and cook for 1 ½ hours {varies depending on the size of the apples}.
   Enjoy with a bowl of vanilla ice cream.

Yields: Six Servings

95.   Apple Dump Cake

Ingredients
Butter {1 stick}
Yellow cake mix {1box}
Apple pie filling {1 can}

Instructions
1. Empty the apple filling into the Crock-Pot®.
2. *Dump* in the mix and then the butter on top of the mix.

Cooking Time: Cook the cake on the low-temperature setting for approximately four hours.
Enjoy!

96.   Chocolate Spoon Cake

Ingredients
1 {1-ounce} small box of Instant chocolate pudding mix
¾ Cups Canola or vegetable oil
1 Box Chocolate Cake Mix {Devil's Food cake is excellent}
1 Cup water
2 Cups sour cream
4 eggs
1 Cup semi-sweet chocolate chips

Instructions
1. Spray the cooker with some cooking oil spray to prevent sticking.
2. Mix all of the ingredients and dump them into the slow cooker—saving the chocolate chips for last.
3. Place the lid on the cooker for four to six hours. Enjoy!

97.   Dump Cake

Ingredients
1 {15-ounces} Box cake mix
2 {21-ounces} Cans of Pie filling {your choice}
1 Tablespoon water
½ Cup {1 stick} Melted butter

Instructions
1. Empty the pie filling into the bottom of the cooker.
2. Combine the cake mix with the water and melted butter, pour it over the filling in the cooker.
3. Cover and cook according to your time table. After the initial time, cook an additional 30 minutes to release the condensation. It is done when you can press the center, and it doesn't 'give' but remains firm.

Spoon into the bowls and enjoy

Yields: Six to Eight servings
Settings: Low for four to five hours or high for two to three hours

Notes: This recipe is prepared in a four-quart cooker. If you use a six-quart cooker, lower the time by one-third.

98.   Fudge in the Cooker

Ingredients
1 {14-ounce} Can sweet condensed milk
1 Tablespoon salted butter
3 Cups semi-sweet chocolate chips
1 teaspoon pure vanilla extract

Other Tools:
9x9 baking pan
Non-stick foil or Parchment paper

Instructions
1. This recipe calls for a four-quart slow cooker. A six-quart will melt faster, so watch the chocolate! Use some cooking spray to layer the cooker and help prevent sticking.
2. Empty everything into the cooker, put the top on, and cook for two hours on low or one on high. Stir every *30* minutes.
3. Once it all forms a liquid, empty it into the container and chill for a minimum of four hours, preferably overnight.
4. Cut into squares.

Yields: Ten to twenty servings

99. Monkey Bread

Ingredients
1 Tube refrigerated biscuits
1 teaspoon cinnamon
¼ Cup butter/margarine melted
1 Cup brown sugar

Instructions
1. Use some kitchen shears to cut each of the biscuits into quarters. Dip them into the melted butter.
2. Roll the pieces through the cinnamon and brown sugar mixture until they are fully covered.
3. Arrange the bread in the bottom of the slow cooker. Toss in the remainder of sugar and cinnamon.
4. Cook two hours and check to see if it is done. You may need to rotate the bottom pieces, from the center to the outside, so it is cooked all the way through.

100. Peach Cobbler

Ingredients
1 white/yellow cake mix
6 large peaches
½ Cup {1 stick} softened butter

Instructions
1. Peel and slice the peaches and place them in the bottom of the cooker.
2. Use a medium mixing bowl, blend the cake mix with the water. Use a pastry blender/potato masher/fork to cut the butter into the cake mix.
3. Sprinkle the mix over the peaches in the slow cooker.
4. Seal the lid and cook.

Serve with a bowl of vanilla ice cream.

Yields: Eight servings
Settings: Low for four hours or high for two to three hours

101. Yogurt in the Slow Cooker

Ingredients
6-Quart Slow Cooker
8 cups {1/2 Gallon whole or 2%} Milk
1 Cup Yogurt {live cultures a must}
1 Unflavored gelatin
1 Towel {large}

Instructions
1. Empty the entire container of milk into the pot and let it cook on low for 2 ½ hours.
2. Unplug the unit and let it rest for three hours.
3. After the time has lapsed, remove two cups of the milk from the pot and whisk ½ cup of the 'live culture' yogurt into the dish. Combine and add the gelatin.
4. Empty the contents into the pot, place the lid on, and wrap the cooker in the towel—letting it rest for eight hours.
5. Chill in some plastic/glass containers and enjoy. Add any additional flavorings you desire, and enjoy.

Note: It will not be the same texture as store bought {not as thick}.
Yields
Settings:

Appetizers and Snacks

102.   Chex Mix

Ingredients
9 Cups Chex Cereal {mixture of wheat, rice, and corn – equal parts}
1 Cup Cheerios
2 Cups Pretzels
1 Cup Peanuts
1 Tablespoon seasoned salt
6 Tablespoons or 1/3 cup hot & melted butter
¼ Cup Worcestershire sauce
Optional: 1 teaspoon garlic powder

Instructions
1. Toss in the peanuts, cheerios, cereal, and pretzels into the slow-cooker pot.
2. In a separate mixing container, whisk the seasoned salt and butter together and blend in the Worcestershire sauce until well mixed
3. Sprinkle the sauce over the top of the ingredients, and toss for about a minute until it is evenly covered.
4. Cook covered for the allotted time stirring at the one, two, and two- and ½ hour intervals, so it doesn't burn.
5. Spread it out on some parchment paper to cool in one layer.
6. This mixture an excellent snack for up to three weeks if you store it in a sealed container.

Cooking Time: Low for three hours

103.   Cocktail Franks – Sweet and Sour

Ingredients
40- ounces pineapple chunks
2 Pounds cocktail franks
1 Cup each:
- Grape jelly
- Chili sauce

3 Tablespoons each:
- Prepared mustard
- Lemon juice

Instructions
1. Mix the jelly, chili sauce, mustard, and lemon juice in the slow cooker, mixing it well.
2. Cover and use the high setting for fifteen to twenty minutes to blend the ingredients
3. Slice the franks into small pieces and toss into the slow cooker.
4. Pour in the drained chunks of pineapple.

Yields: Ten Servings
Cooking Times: The low setting for four hours or the high setting for two hours

104.   Spicy BBQ Kielbasa

Ingredients
2 Pounds Kielbasa
½ Cup light brown sugar
2 Cups ketchup
1 teaspoon hot sauce
2 teaspoons Creole mustard
1 Tablespoon Worcestershire sauce
1 finely chopped medium onion
½ Cup Bourbon

Instructions

1. Cut the kielbasa into ½-inch rounds
2. Mix all of the components of the recipe into the crock pot.
3. Place the lid on the pot and cook on set the timer for four to five hours.
4. Serve them on a platter with some toothpicks or in a dish to the side.

Have Fun!

105.   Cajun Boiled Peanuts

Ingredients
8 Cups water to start
1 Pound {in the shell} raw peanuts
1 Tablespoon garlic powder
1 {3-ounce} package crab boil {Shrimp Boil or Zatarain's}
½ Cup salt
2 Tablespoons each

- Red pepper flakes
- Cajun seasoning

Instructions

1. Toss the peanuts and water to the crock pot. Toss in the Cajun seasoning, red pepper flakes, salt, and garlic powder.
2. Next, add the crab boil and cook for 12 to 24 hours on low.
3. Add water as needed to keep the nuts covered. Use a slotted spoon to serve them up.

Note: The longer they cook, the stronger the flavor will be in the nut.

Dips

106.   Beer Cheese Dip

Ingredients
½ Cup beer
1 Lb. Processed cheese spread
¼ teaspoon Tabasco sauce

Tasty Sides:
- Baked French fries
- Veggies
- Tortilla chips

Instructions
1. Cut the cheese spread into cubes.
2. Combine the first three ingredients in a one to two-quart slow cooker.
3. Cover the pot and cook for 40 minutes until the cheese melts on the high setting.
4. Scrape the sides with a spatula and continue stirring until smooth.
5. Lower the heat, and it will be awesome for about four hours, stirring every so often.

Use your favorite dipper of bell pepper strips, celery sticks, or baby carrots. The sky is the limit! Have a Party!

107.   Buffalo Chicken Dip

Ingredients
2 to 3 {12-13ounces} Cans Chicken breast in water or
                    2 to 3 Chicken breasts {12 to 13 ounces}
2 packages cream cheese
1 {10-ounces} bottle ranch dressing
1 scant cup shredded cheddar cheese
6 ounces red hot buffalo sauce {Franks is awesome}

Instructions
1. Combine everything {omit the shredded cheese for now}
    in the lightly sprayed slow cooker and cook for about 45
    minutes using the high setting.
2. Stir occasionally, lower the heat to the low setting and
    continue to cook the mixture.
3. Stir in the cheese right before you are ready to serve the
    tasty treat.

Have plenty of tortilla chips around and serve it right out of the
pot to keep it hot!

Sweet Stuff {Appetizers}

108.   Candied Pecans

Ingredients
4 Cups pecans/almonds/walnuts/cashews {or a mix}
1 Cup sugar
½ Cup brown sugar
1 ½ Tablespoons cinnamon
2 teaspoons vanilla
1 egg white
¼ Cup water

Instructions

1. Use a large dish to combine the cinnamon, sugar, and brown sugar, and set it to the side.
2. In another bowl, whisk the vanilla and egg whites until they become frothy.
3. Spray the slow cooker with some nonstick cooking spray and add the chosen nuts. Pour in the egg mix and stir until they are covered.
4. Add the sugar {step 1} and stir.
5. Cook for 3 hours—stirring every twenty minutes.
6. The last 20 minutes, pour in ¼ cup of water to the cooker to make the outer shell crunchy.

Note: This was prepared in a 4 ½ Quart Crockpot

Chapter 6: Beverages

109. Apple Cider

Ingredients
2 {3-inch} cinnamon sticks
2 quarts apple cider
½ Cup packed brown sugar
1 teaspoon each:
- Whole allspice
- Whole cloves

1 sliced orange
Cheesecloth

Instructions
1. Arrange the allspice, cloves, and cinnamon in a double-thick layer of cheesecloth, tying with a string to make a spice sack.
2. Empty the brown sugar and cider into a three-quart cooker, stirring until the sugar is dissolved. Drop in the spice bag.
3. Arrange the orange slices on the top of the arrangement; cover and cook until thoroughly heated.
4. Dispose of the spice bag.

Yields: Eight Servings {2 quarts}
Preparation time: five minutes
Cooking time: two hours

110.   Berry Lemonade

Ingredients
1 {12-ounces) Package frozen mixed berries
12 tea bags {regular sized}
5 Cups cold natural refrigerated lemonade
8 Cups water
1/3 Cup honey
For serving: 2 Lemons cut into 6 slices

Instructions
1. Discard the paper tags from the bags and put them in with all of the ingredients {omit the lemon slices}.
2. Use a 5-quart slow cooker and cover on low for three hours.
3. Empty the tea into a dish and discard the solid ingredients.
4. Serve either over ice or warm. Dress them up with a lemon slice or two.

Yields: Twelve Servings of 1 lemon slice and 1 cup of tea

111. Caramel Apple Cider

Ingredients
1 Cup caramel flavoring syrup
8 cups apple juice or cider
¼ Cup lemon juice
2 {3-inches) cinnamon sticks
1 Vanilla bean
1 Tablespoon whole allspice

Possible Toppings
- Cinnamon Sticks
- Whipped Cream
- Hot Caramel Ice cream topping

Instructions
1. Use a 3-quart cooker to combine the lemon juice, caramel syrup, and apple cider.
2. Split the vanilla bean, scrape the seeds and add to the mixture.
3. Use a doubled piece of cheesecloth to add the allspice, cinnamon sticks, and the bean, tying it with some string forming a bag. Add to the pot
4. Cover and cook until thoroughly heated for about two to three hours on the low setting.
5. Pour the cider into mugs and relax.

Yields: 12 Servings {3/4 Cup each}

112.   Solo Lemonade

Ingredients
3 Cups fresh lemon juice {approximately a dozen lemons}
4 Cups water
¼ Cup honey
1 ¾ to 2 Cups sugar
Cinnamon Sticks

Instructions
1. Hold the cinnamon sticks, but add everything else into a 3 or 3 ½ quart slow cooker.
2. Place the lid on the pot, and cook for three hours using the low function or until warm.
3. Whisk thoroughly before serving. Serve with the cinnamon sticks.

Note: If you do not have the time to fresh-squeeze the lemons, you can substitute a lemon juice concentrate.

Yields: Nine cups

113.   Mocha Hot Chocolate

Ingredients
3 C. 2% Reduced-fat milk
1 {1 ½ quarts} chocolate light ice cream
2 Tablespoons instant espresso granules

Instructions
1. Add the ice cream into a three-quart slow cooker. Empty the milk and the espresso. Put the lid on the cooker for three hours on the low setting.
2. Use a ladle to serve the hot chocolate into an awaiting mug.

Yields: 9 Servings – 2/3 cups each

114.   **Nutella Hot Chocolate**

Ingredients
6 ½ Cups skim milk
1 {14-ounce} Can sweetened condensed milk
1 Cup Nutella
¼ teaspoon salt
1 Tablespoons vanilla extract
¼ Cup unsweetened cocoa powder

Instructions
1. Use some cooking spray to prep the slow cooker.
2. Add the ingredients to the pot and stir.
3. Place the lid on the cooker and heat on the low setting for two hours.
4. Whisk it about before serving!

Yields: Six to Eight Servings

115.   **Spiced Pear Cider**

For those hot days, prepare this ahead of time and chill!

Ingredients
8 whole cloves
16 - Whole allspice
4 {3-inch} cinnamon sticks
2 Cups pear nectar
6 Cups unsweetened pear juice

Instructions
1. Prepare an 8-inch square of cheesecloth or a coffee filter with the cinnamon, cloves, and allspice. Use a string to make a sack and add it to the cooker along with the rest of the ingredients.
2. Cover with the top and cook for three hours on the low setting.

Yields: 1 Cup Serving size {Recipe for 8 cups}

116.   **Wassail Bowl Punch**

Think of this 'warming to the bone' drink the next time you have to shovel the driveway and are chilled!

Ingredients
2 Cups Orange juice
4 Cups Each:
- Cranberry juice
- Hot brewed tea
- Unsweetened apple juice

1 Cup sugar
3 {3-inch} Cinnamon sticks
¾ Cup lemon juice
12 whole cloves

Instructions
1. This beverage calls for a 5-quart slow cooker. Add the tea, orange juice, apple juice, sugar, lemon juice, and cranberry juice to the slow cooker.
2. In a piece of double-thick cheesecloth, combine the cloves and cinnamon sticks, tying with a string to make a bag, and add to the combination in the cooker.
3. Place the lid on the pot and cook for one hour on high. If the punch boils, it is done.

Yields: 14 Tasty servings {3 ½ quarts}

Boozy Drinks

117.   Lemon Ginger Hot Toddies

Ingredients
2 Cups fresh lemon juice {Approximately 14 small lemons}
8 Cups water
5 Tablespoons finely chopped crystallized ginger
2 Cups honey
1 {3-inch} piece peeled ginger

Instructions
1. Cut the ginger into ¼-inch slices
2. Add the first five ingredients into the cooker, and place on high for four hours {covered}.
3. Throw the ginger away. Pour in the brandy and rum. Empty into the mugs and garnish with the lemon rinds if you choose.

Yields: 1 Cup Size for 14 Servings

118.   Hot Mocha Spirits

This recipe provides an invite for the cooker to be a hit at the party—straight from the pot!

Ingredients
6 {1-ounce} semisweet chopped baking squares
        Or 1 {6-ounce package} semisweet chocolate mini-morsels
8 Cups milk
¼ Cup instant coffee granules
½ Cup powdered sugar
1 Cup Brandy
Optional Garnishes:
- Grated semisweet chocolate
- Sweetened whipped cream

Instructions
1. In a four-quart slow cooker, add the first five ingredients.
2. Place the lid on the cooker and cook for four to five hours on low until the chocolate is melted. Whisk it around the two- hour mark. Be sure to give it a good whisk before serving.
3. Garnish as desired.

Yields: Ten Cups

119.   Mulled Wine

Ingredients
1 C. apple cider
1 C. cranberry juice
1 bottle red wine
1 C. fresh cranberries
1/3 C. sugar
2 oranges {juice and peels}
1 Tbsp. Whole cloves
2 whole cinnamon sticks
1 Tbsp. star anise

Instructions
1. Combine everything in the slow cooker, stirring well to combine.
2. Cook for around 30 minutes on the high setting.
3. Garnish each glass with a slice of orange peel on the edge of the warm drink.

Yields: Four Servings

120.   Viennese Coffee

Ingredients
3 Tablespoons chocolate syrup
3 Cups Strong brewed coffee
1/3 Cup heavy whipping cream
1 teaspoon sugar
¼ Cup Irish Cream liqueur or crème de cacao
Optional: Whipped Cream & Chocolate curls

Instructions
1. Combine the syrup, sugar, and coffee in a 1 to 1 ½ quart slow cooker.
2. Cover the pot and cook for 2 ½ hours on the low setting.
3. Blend in the crème de cacao/liqueur and the whipping cream. Replace the lid and cook another thirty minutes or so until warmed.

Yields: Four Servings

Conclusion

If you have a busy lifestyle and just don't have the extra time to cater to the kitchen with meal preparation, your personal copy of *The All-American Slow Cooker Cookbook* will save the day.

Let's hope it was informative and provided you with many new ways to use your slow cooker. The next step is to take some time out of your busy schedule and check out some of these scrumptious dishes.

Your family will surely appreciate the extra goodies. You will find so many delicious recipes that you will consider "effortless" when you see they have such a short amount of preparation time. Why not have a party and show off a bit? Now let's see how good you are with your slow cooker!

Index

Chapter 1: Breakfast

The Sweets Corner

Chapter 2: Lunch Favorites

New York Dirty Hot Dogs
Beef

Chicken

Turkey

Pork
- Pork Barbecue
- Root Beer Pulled Pork

Chapter 3: Soups, Sides, Veggies and Casseroles

Soups
- Bean Soup
- Caribbean Beef Stew
- Crock-Pot® Taco Soup

Special Instant Pot - Slow-Cooker Soups
- Butternut Squash & Curry Soup
- Indo-Chinese Corn Soup
- Instant Pot Saag
- Split Pea Soup
- 3-Bean Chili
- Veggie & Lentil Soup

Noodle Time
- Lasagna Enchantment
- Macaroni and Cheese
- Beef Stroganoff

Chicken, Beef, and Pork Casseroles
- Chicken with Mushrooms and Artichokes
- Crock-Pot Dinner: Beef or Chicken
- Swiss Steak Supper

Veggies
- Bourbon Baked Beans
- Corn on the Cob
- Ranch Mushrooms
- Stuffed Banana Peppers
- Slow Cooked Baked Potatoes
- Sweet Potatoes

- Sweet Potato Casserole

Chapter 4: Dinner Favorites

- **Corned Beef**
- **Corned Beef and Cabbage**

Beef
- Beef Burgundy with Noodles
- Beef Tips
- Meatloaf: Turkey or Beef
- Mississippi Roast
- Steaks in the Pot
- Steak Pizzaiola

Chicken
- Barbecue Chicken
- Beer and Barbecue Chicken
- Buffalo Chicken
- Butter Ranch Chicken
- Chicken Stock
- Crock Pot Chicken
- Creamy Chicken with Biscuits
-      Biscuits for the Chicken {Above}
- Caesar Chicken
- Chicken and Dumplings
- Chicken and Mushroom Gravy
- Cranberry Chicken
- French Onion Chicken
- Hawaiian Chicken
- Honey Mustard Chicken
- Italian Style Chicken
- Mexican Chicken
- Orange Soda Chicken
- Rotisserie-Style Chicken
- Sweet and Sour Chicken

- Swedish Meatballs
- Teriyaki Chicken

Turkey

- Stuffed – Roasted Turkey

Fish

- Citrus Flavored Fish
- Lemon Pepper Tilapia with Asparagus
- Salmon Bake
- Shrimp Scampi

Pork

- BBQ Style Pork Steaks
- Maple Orange Pork Shoulder
- Pastured Pork Shoulder
- Pepsi® Roast
- Ranch Pork Chops
- Squash 'N Chops
- Sweet Pork

Ham

- Maple Pineapple Ham
- Ham with Cider Gravy

Chapter 5: Desserts & Appetizers

- Applesauce
- Apple Crisp
- Apple Dump Cake
- Chocolate Spoon Cake
- Dump Cake
- Fudge in the Cooker
- Monkey Bread

- Peach Cobbler
- Yogurt in the Slow Cooker

Appetizers and Snacks
- Chex Mix
- Cocktail Franks – Sweet and Sour
- Spicy BBQ Kielbasa
- Cajun Boiled Peanuts

Dips
- Beer Cheese Dip
- Buffalo Chicken Dip

Sweet Stuff {Appetizers}
- Candied Pecans

Chapter 6: Beverages
- Apple Cider
- Berry Lemonade
- Caramel Apple Cider
- Solo Lemonade
- Mocha Hot Chocolate
- Nutella Hot Chocolate
- Spiced Pear Cider
- Wassail Bowl Punch

Boozy Drinks
- Lemon Ginger Hot Toddies
- Hot Mocha Spirits
- Mulled Wine
- Viennese Coffee

62476247R00066

Made in the USA
Lexington, KY
11 April 2017